THE
POWER
OF
POSITIVE
CONFESSION

VOLUME 2

MATTHEW ASHIMOLOWO

MATTYSON
MEDIA

Mattyson Media Company
P. O. Box 12961
London
E15 1UR

Bible quotes are from the King James Bible unless otherwise stated.

ISBN 1-874646-20-1

Contents

ABUNDANCE

KEY SCRIPTURE - EPHESIANS 3:20

"Now unto him that is able to do exceeding abundantly above all that we ask or think, according to the power that worketh in us."

I believe and confess that God's abundance flows into my life. The Lord will do exceedingly great things in my life, for the breakthrough of abundance beyond my imagination rests upon my life. I shall experience blessing in every area of my business and home. The grace of God abounds unto me, the Lord opens unto me His abundant treasure. The Lord causes long-suffering and goodness that is abundant towards me to increase.

I boldly command every hidden treasure of abundance to be exposed to me that the riches of the ungodly will enter into my hand for favour and blessing. I shall know the grace of God without trouble. I believe and confess that the Lord anoints my eyes to see the hidden riches of this world. He causes creativity to flow in my life and business, my ears are anointed to hear what God is saying, my eyes are anointed to see what God has in store, my hands are anointed to touch the blessings set aside for me. There shall be an outbreak of the rain of God's favour in my life. For the Lord will cause my life to be exceedingly blessed. The Lord will cause me to enter His great favour.

I boldly confess that God makes my spiritual life good and fruitful. He causes prosperity on my business and ventures. I receive wisdom, knowledge and divine creativity to excel in life. I boldly declare that I become a point of reference to the glory of God for the Lord causes me to increase even in the midst of my tribulation. Tribulation will produce an eternal weight of glory.

I boldly declare that the Lord will command every drought and famine area in my life to be transformed to abundance. He will cause His contentment to be upon me. The blessings of Zion flows into my life. The grace of sufficiency abounds unto me.

I am blessed and highly favoured.

ACCOMPLISHMENT

KEY SCRIPTURE - PROVERBS 13:19

"The desire accomplished is sweet to the soul: but it is abomination to fools to depart from evil."

I believe and confess that the Lord is good. His faithfulness is to all generations. He causes me to be fruitful in all my labour and crowns me with good success.

I believe and confess that everything I start, finishes well. God's grace abounds on to me as I carry out His vision for my life. The projects I initiate will be accomplished.

He who started a good thing in me, will be faithful to complete it.

My targeted goals shall be reached. I shall attain my calling and the grace of the Lord shall be sufficient for me for He will give me courage to win in all situations so that fruitfulness follows all my labour and good success follows all my effort.

I am blessed and highly favoured.

AFFECTION

KEY SCRIPTURE - ROMANS 12:10

"Be kindly affectioned one to another with brotherly love; in honour preferring one another;"

I believe and confess that the grace of God abounds unto me. God has deposited in me His unconditional love. The blood of Jesus has drawn me closer to the throne of grace.

The love of God flows from me to other people at all times. I am free from hatred. There is no trace of hypocrisy in me. The God-kind of affection operates in me and through me. My life, ministry and relationships are motivated by genuine affection. I refuse to allow the hurts of the past to stop the love of God from flowing through me.

For the Lord Himself anoints my eyes to see those who need my love and gives me the grace to reach out to even the unlovable. By faith I confess that the ability to flow in unconditional love works in me. God gives me the grace to be an example of His overflowing love and an example of giving forgiveness to the unforgivable.

I am blessed and highly favoured.

ANOINTING

KEY SCRIPTURE - ISAIAH 10:27

"And it shall come to pass in that day, that his burden shall be taken away from off thy shoulder, and his yoke from off thy neck, and the yoke shall be destroyed because of the anointing."

I give praise to God for His divine ability. I thank God because His grace is sufficient for me at all times. He gives me confidence to face each moment.

I believe and confess that the anointing of the Holy Spirit, which remove bondage and destroy yokes, resides in me. Through me the joy of the Lord is released to those who lack it. I am anointed to subdue nations for God. The power of God resides in me to withstand the evil weapons of the enemy.

By faith I confess that the anointing of God makes the difference in my ministry. Therefore, I am anointed to bring good tidings to those who are in need and set free people in emotional prisons.

I boldly confess that I am a prophetic voice to my generation. The word of the Lord in my mouth shall be anointed.

I am blessed and highly favoured.

ANXIETY

KEY SCRIPTURE - Philippians 4:6

"Be careful for nothing; but in every thing by prayer and supplication with thanksgiving let your requests be made known unto God."

I thank the Lord for His joy that passes understanding which flows through me. I have been set free from the tendency of worry and anxiety, in the name of the Lord. I am not afraid of the future, because my Father goes ahead of me.

I believe and confess that God has set me free from every form of emotional bondage and has filled me with godly confidence.

I boldly declare that I shall not bring forth for trouble, nor gather my possessions for the day of adversity. The load of care that the enemy placed on me is broken, in Jesus name.

I believe and confess that fear and worry are not my possessions. For all my worries I receive boldness and a sound mind. I am filled with the love of God. My future is as certain and bright as the promises of God.

I am blessed and highly favoured.

ATTAINMENT

Key Scripture - Philippians 3:11-12

"If by any means I might attain unto the resurrection of the dead.

Not as though I had already attained, either were already perfect: but I follow after, if that I may apprehend that for which also I am apprehended of Christ Jesus."

I believe and confess that the Lord is good. His faithfulness extends to the heavens. God is my Father and He provides all my needs through Christ Jesus.

By faith I present all challenges to Him and boldly declare that I have victory through Him.

I believe and confess that I have received the anointing to prosper. I have been broken free from the spirit and control of poverty. My blessings which the enemy has hindered have been released right now. The stronghold of satan have been destroyed right now. I will attain God's purpose and destiny for me.

For the Lord Himself causes me to achieve my destiny. He gives me motivation to reach my purpose to His glory. I confess that I will make it to the prize of my high calling. I thank the Lord because He shall cause me to stand in His sanctuary and testify of His strength. I shall come through all challenges to give testimonies. For the Lord will cause me to advance in achieving my purpose.

I am blessed and highly favoured.

ATTITUDE

KEY SCRIPTURE - ROMANS 12:11

"Not slothful in business; fervent in spirit; serving the Lord;"

I believe and confess that the Lord is good, for He has changed my mourning into dancing. He has given me a reason to laugh in life, no matter what I go through.

I believe and confess that it will be all right, for the Lord shall be my strength and encouragement for the light and darkness of this world.

I believe and confess that no matter what I go through, and in the face of discouragement, only the purpose and counsel of God will stand. Neglect of the past will become my stepping-stone. The limitation I have known will become my source of breakthrough. Every satanic limitation is destroyed, in the name of the Lord. Every persecution I face will result in promotion.

I believe and confess that every negative attitude of the past is being uprooted and the Lord is causing me to have a single minded commitment to His purpose and will. I rejoice in the face of discouragement for the Lord makes my eyes to be set towards heaven like a flint and my feet to run like a deer. By faith I confess that every evil curse pronounced against me shall not stand and the Lord uses me to be a repairer of the breech between those who are offended.

I am blessed and highly favoured.

BARRENNESS

KEY SCRIPTURE - DEUTERONOMY 7:14

"Thou shalt be blessed above all people: there shall not be male or female barren among you, or among your cattle."

I believe and confess that the Lord is good and He is faithful to make His promise good.

I thank the Lord because He will not withhold from me any good thing. Every manifestation of barrenness is disappearing, in the name of Jesus. Barrenness has ceased in my life, in the name of Jesus. I shall be fruitful in all areas. Out of my barrenness shall come forth the miracle people, the miracle job, the miracle of all that brings glory to the name of the Lord. My heart is released from the bondage of barrenness. Every aspect of my life shall keep bearing fruit, for the Lord will restore all my lost resources.

I boldly declare that I conceive with the right seed, vision and ideas. I shall be surrounded by the fruit of my confession. The Lord has put a song of victory in my mouth, for I shall not be unfruitful or barren.

By faith I confess and renounce every sin and mistake that has caused my barrenness. I reach forth and receive the miracle God has for me. By faith I confess that I have victory and my children shall possess the gates of their enemies. For the Lord will cause His miracle to happen in my life and every area of dryness shall become an area of fruitfulness. I believe and confess that I shall conceive the right seed, the right vision and the right idea, and I shall not miscarry the purpose and the pregnancy which God has given me.

I am blessed and highly favoured.

BLESSING

KEY SCRIPTURE - EpHESIANS 1:3

"Blessed be the God and Father of our Lord Jesus Christ, who hath blessed us with all spiritual blessings in heavenly places in Christ:"

I believe and confess that the Lord is good. His manifold blessings are made known to those who trust Him. God always causes me to have victory through the Lord Jesus, according to His Word. The Lord will favour me with all round blessing which cannot be overlooked.

Every evil pronouncement militating against my life is cancelled with the blood. I break the generational curse that is militating against my understanding. I come against every limitation which the enemy is trying to put on my life.

I boldly confess the blessing of the Lord's favour and financial blessing, in Jesus Name. I receive God's divine endorsement and proclaim God's divine endorsement now, in all that I do. For the Lord will favour me with His divine direction. All my hidden blessings are being exposed by the Lord. The manifestation of God's blessing shall erase the days of sorrow.

I am blessed and highly favoured.

BREAKING THE

CURSE

KEY SCRIPTURE - GALATIANS 3:13

*"Christ hath redeemed us from the curse of the law,
being made a curse for us: for it is written, Cursed is
every one that hangeth on a tree:"*

I believe and confess that the Lord is good for He
has redeemed me from the curse of the law. By faith I
confess that the curse of disobedience to parents over my
life is broken in the name of Jesus. Every contrary law of
the enemy over me is destroyed in the name of the Lord.
The effect of economic and financial dealing that is false
is cancelled in the name of Jesus.

I break the curse of sickness, the curse of disease,
poverty and lack that dates back to four generations in my
family, in the name of Jesus. I cancel the impact of
incestuous experience. I cancel the impact of
disobedience to God, idolatry and every form of
generational curse that is hindering me from entering the

purpose of God for my life.

I believe and confess that I am free from the yoke of bondage. I believe and confess that I am free from the curse that makes a family down trodden. Slavery is not my portion.

Sickness is not my portion, disease is rejected in my life in the name of Jesus. Every hold of the enemy is broken. Evil pronouncements made into my life are cancelled in the name of Jesus. I thank the Lord in advance for turning every curse into a blessing and every challenge into His favour in Jesus name.

CHANGE

KEY SCRIPTURE - Job 14:14

*"If a man die, shall he live again? All the days of my
appointed time will I wait, till my change come."*

I believe and confess that the Lord is good and His
grace abounds on to me.

By faith I receive His grace to see transformation in
every area of my life. He has taken away hindrances from
my way. I pull down the strongholds of the mind and
every form of imagination which contradicts the Word of
God.

By faith I confess that I overcome fleshly devices
and bring them under the subjection of the Holy Spirit.
In place of hatred I am filled with the love of God and in
place of all darkness the light of the word enlightens my
faith.

I believe and confess that the faith to overcome
problems works in me. For the Lord causes me to be
blessed wherever I go. God is working in me and doing a
new thing. I shall not be overcome by criticism or
negative jealous people but the grace of Jesus Christ

continues to work and produce humility in me. By faith I take authority over every strong man that binds me and I declare my liberty in Jesus Christ and say I am growing and going higher. The word of God enlightens my path from day to day in Jesus name.

I am blessed and highly favoured.

CHEERFULNESS

KEY SCRIPTURE - PROVERBS 15:13

*"A merry heart maketh a cheerful countenance: but by
sorrow of the heart the spirit is broken."*

I believe and confess that my spirit is being lifted up
and God causes me to rejoice. Even in the face of adversity, I
receive His help to find joy in the time of trouble.

In the face of an impossible situation, I confess that
it shall turn to testimony, for the Lord will turn to joy that
which the enemy has brought against me. The joy of the
Lord which flows from my life shall be a testimony to
those who see me.

I believe and confess that the joy of the Lord overflows
from me and brings encouragement to others. The cloud
of discouragement is broken in my life. Worry has no control
over me. I receive boldness to rejoice in the face of adversity.
I glory in the Lord and my saviour who has filled my heart
with joy and my mouth with a new song. I declare that I
shall be joyful in the midst of my temporary setbacks for
He gives me boldness to dance and walk upon my storms.

I am blessed and highly favoured.

COMFORT

KEY SCRIPTURE - 2 CORINTHIANS 1:4

"Who comforteth us in all our tribulation, that we may be able to comfort them which are in any trouble, by the comfort wherewith we ourselves are comforted of God."

I bless the name of the Lord, because He is good. I thank the Lord for He hears me when I call Him.

By faith I receive the strength of the Lord who is the Father of all comforts. His grace and power shall be sufficient for me in every situation. He helps me to rise against every tribulation and establishes me in the times of setbacks.

I believe and confess that every grief and worry is dispelled in the name of Jesus Christ. My life is strengthened to minister to others and to show them the comfort of the Lord.

I believe and confess that the Lord has made me an instrument of comfort to those who are in trouble. He has chosen me to break the hold of satanic bondage in the life of those in trouble. By faith I confess that every tendency to walk in worry is removed from my life. The peace of God that passes understanding garrisons my heart and makes me to rejoice in the midst of affliction and to declare the comfort of the Lord that surrounds me. My heart is filled with the constant comfort of the Holy Spirit and I sing of the victory I have in God.

I am blessed and highly favoured.

COMMITMENT

KEY SCRIPTURE - PROVERbS 3:5

"Trust in the LORD with all thine heart; and lean not unto thine own understanding."

I believe and confess that I am a child of God, committed to doing His will on earth. I receive grace to achieve my goals and visions. I will fulfil my purpose on earth. God's mighty hand upholds me and strengthens me to be faithful to the end.

I reject discouragement, carnal tendency and everything that wants to stop me. My eyes are anointed to see the tricks of the devil and to overcome. I am totally yielded to do the will of God. God has begun a good thing in me and He will equip me to finish well.

I boldly declare that I resist everything that tries to stop me from reaching my goal. I confess that I began well and I shall finish well. I reject and refuse every spirit of discouragement in the name of the Lord. I will not go back to the things I have forsaken but shall move on from glory to glory. My life will bring a testimony to the name of Jesus Christ.

I am blessed and highly favoured.

COMPASSION

KEY SCRIPTURE - PSALM 111:4

*"He hath made his wonderful works to be remembered:
the LORD is gracious and full of compassion."*

I believe and confess that the Lord is good. I thank
the Lord for a heart of compassion towards the needy. I
give God praise for He has not consumed us because of
His compassion. I bless the name of the Lord for
providing mercy until mercy abounds in my life.

By faith, I confess that forgiveness and compassion
will flow to His people from His throne. I boldly confess
that God's grace brings salvation to me and to all my
household. The compassion of the Lord will result in
ministering to the hurting people. The compassion of the
Lord will flow through me and make a way to those who
need to know the love of God.

By faith, I confess that the Lord will lead those who
will minister to me to come my way. I receive God's
mercy and compassion for every situation that I may be
in. I speak by faith that the Lord will expose every
imminent danger to me in Jesus name. I boldly confess

that my ministry will flow out of a heart of compassion and mercy.

I boldly confess that the place of my captivity will turn to the place of the manifestation of God's compassion and in the midst of peoples abandonment and departure from me, I will know the abundance of God's love. I bless the name of the Lord for He has promised not to forget me or forsake me. I thank the Lord because nothing will hinder His love to me.

I give God praise for the restoration of everything which I have lost.

I am blessed and highly favoured.

CONCENTRATION

Key Scripture - Hebrews 12:2

*"Looking unto Jesus the author and finisher of [our]
faith; who for the joy that was set before him endured
the cross, despising the shame, and is set down at the
right hand of the throne of God."*

I give God the praise for His continuous leading in
my life. I thank the Lord for helping me to locate His
programme for my life.

God gives me the grace to forget the mistakes of the
past and every evil destructive element. I receive boldness
to be happy in the midst of setback and overcome the
spirit of discouragement.

I boldly confess that I am focused on my goals. I
have received grace to possess my possession. I keep my
eyes on finishing the race as I arise to my destiny and calling.

I take authority over every destructive element in my
life and I command such elements to depart in the name of
the Lord. I confess by faith my happiness in the midst of setback.
I receive Gods grace to push on and to possess my possession.
No evil befalls me. My eyes are set on the Lord and the
goals before me. I have begun and I shall finish my race.

I am blessed and highly favoured.

CONFIDENCE

KEY SCRIPTURE - HEBREWS 10:35

"Cast not away therefore your confidence, which hath great recompence of reward."

I believe and confess that the grace and favour of the Lord abounds to me. God gives me the confidence and boldness to be a witness for Him. Anything I bind or loose shall be as I declare, in Jesus name. I have the authority of God over the attacks of the enemy. I refuse to be bound by the spirit of fear of men.

I boldly declare that I shall stand in the times of setbacks and overcome the arrows of the enemy until my change comes.

By faith, I declare that every wall the enemy places against me crumbles, in the name of Jesus. I shall see the downfall of satan and live in total victory throughout my Christian race.

By faith I confess that every mouth that rises against me in judgement is condemned. I refuse to bow or to be bound by the fear of men. My confidence is in the Lord who has made all things well on my behalf. By faith I declare my victory over the fiery arrow of the enemy and I tear down every wall that the enemy is trying to build against me. Walls of limitation shall not hold me down; rather the ability of the Lord dwells in me and helps me to excel in everything I do.

I am blessed and highly favoured.

CONSECRATION

KEY SCRIPTURE - ROMANS 12:1-2

"I beseech you therefore, brethren, by the mercies of God, that ye present your bodies a living sacrifice, holy, acceptable unto God, which is your reasonable service.

And be not conformed to this world: but be ye transformed by the renewing of your mind, that ye may prove what is that good, and acceptable, and perfect, will of God."

I believe and confess that the Lord is good. His faithfulness endures forever. I receive His grace to live a godly life. I am committed to live for Jesus. By faith I receive the ability to live victorious in the face of temptation.

I boldly confess that all that I do will bring honour to the name of the Lord. My body is yielded to the service of the Lord. My mind is renewed by the Word of God. The Holy Spirit lives in me. Sin has no dominion over me. I have a testimony of holy living. I am free from spiritual bondage to serve the Lord with a godly heart.

I give God praise for counting me worthy to be among His chosen generation. By faith I make a commitment today to consecrate my life to Him. Flesh shall not conquer me or hold me in bondage. I reject the tendency to walk in sin and unrighteousness. I loose myself from all the things that tend to bind me in the name of the Lord. I rejoice in the Lord for supplying the grace to walk in the light and in His word at all times. I boldly declare that I am the righteousness of God, a brand new creature in Jesus Christ.

I am blessed and highly favoured.

COURAGE

KEY SCRIPTURE - JOSHUA 1:7

"Only be thou strong and very courageous, that thou mayest observe to do according to all the law, which Moses my servant commanded thee: turn not from it to the right hand or to the left, that thou mayest prosper whithersoever thou goest."

I believe and confess that the Lord gives me courage to overcome every challenge that I face.

I boldly declare that the presence of the Lord goes with me into all situations. The promise of the Lord is good for me, no matter what I face, and the grace of the Lord strengthens me everyday.

I boldly take back what the enemy has stolen, because my eyes are anointed to see the strategies of the enemy and to say no to the subtle lies of satan.

I believe and confess that I shall act courageously in the face of challenges, for the Lord will go before me to win all my battles. They that are for me are greater than those who are against me for the battle is not over until I win.

By faith, I take authority over the spirit of fear and

bind it from controlling me. I take authority over the plan of the enemy and declare my victory ahead of every battle in the name of the Lord. I rejoice in the Lord for He has given me the courage to stand and face every overwhelming temptation. No trouble befalls me and no danger overcomes me. He gives courage and strength to finish my race and in my weakness, He makes me strong. The grace of Jesus Christ increases unto me day by day.

I am blessed and highly favoured.

DECISION

Key Scripture - Proverbs 16:33

"The lot is cast into the lap; but the whole disposing thereof is of the LORD."

I believe and confess that the Lord is good and He directs my path daily. The Lord is on my side. He opens my eyes to know His ways.

I boldly confess that God anoints my mind to make good decisions. Every counsel taken against my wellbeing shall not stand, for my eyes shall be anointed to know time-wasting decisions and to reject procrastination. I give God praise for I shall be led by Him at all times.

By faith I declare that my mind is clear from every confusion and at the cross road of life, the manifestation of the spirit of confusion shall not be in my life; rather I boldly declare that the counsel of the Lord concerning my life will be established and the Lord anoints my eyes to see and to know time wasting decisions. Everything I do, everything I touch shall be blessed of the Lord for He guides my steps. My steps are ordered of Him, I shall not fall in Jesus name.

I am blessed and highly favoured.

DELIVERANCE

Key Scripture - Obadiah 1:17

"But upon mount Zion shall be deliverance, and there shall be holiness; and the house of Jacob shall possess their possessions."

I believe and confess that the Lord is good, for I am delivered from the trap of the enemy. The Son of God sets me free and I am free indeed. No evil befalls me. No weapon formed against me prospers.

Every arrow of satan falls for my sake, and every bondage of the devil is cancelled, in Jesus name. The curse of idolatry is broken in my life. The curse from generation sins is broken, in Jesus name.

Christ has redeemed me from the curse of the law. I am free from the power of the evil one. My freedom is guaranteed in Jesus. I am covered by His precious blood.

By faith I rejoice for the Lord has set me free from every tendency of a desperate spirit. The Lord has set me free from a spirit of competition. I am broken free from the spirit of confrontation. No demon of seduction holds me in bondage. I rejoice in the Lord because uncontrollable jealousy is no longer my portion. The grace of Jesus Christ gives me power to stay away from all associations that are of compromise. By faith I declare my deliverance from every trap of satan. God causes me to walk in victory and not in defeat and therefore, every bondage of the enemy is broken. By faith, I declare that the grace of Jesus Christ and His mercy is manifest in my life at all times. I confess that in the midst of my setback, I shall yet sing of God deliverance. For the Lord causes me to have victory over every generational curse. Today there is a cancellation in my life of every seed of the enemy and Gods deliverance power flows daily in my life.

I boldly declare that every curse of disobedience is nullified by the word of God. The curse of the enemy extending on my work, on my business and on my family is cancelled from this day. My life, my home, my work, my future and my destiny is covered by the blood of Jesus. I shall be safe in the land.

I am blessed and highly favoured.

DIFFICULT PEOPLE

KEY SCRIPTURE - Ephesians 1:22

"And hath put all things under his feet, and gave him to be the head over all things to the church,"

I believe and confess that God is good. His faithfulness extends to the heavens. I give God praise because He gives me wisdom to handle people who are difficult. I bless the name of the Lord for giving me victory over every satanic lie.

I confess by faith that the dishonest are exposed and that those who mean evil against my life are exposed by the Holy Spirit. I am free from the fear of man. I am victorious over impossible people.

By faith I receive boldness to confront those who deliberately cause fear and panic. I reject the works of the enemy and confess that I have received wisdom to handle those who make unnecessary demands on my life. I have received wisdom to deal with the difficult, for the spirit of the Lord anoints my eyes to see the fake and the truthful.

My eyes are anointed to see the plans of the enemy. My heart is filled with wisdom to handle every situation. No evil, danger, or weapon formed against me prospers for the Lord exposes every false brother. Those who belittle me shall see me make progress.

The blood of Jesus covers me against every critical spirit, against the spirit of jealousy and against every conspirator who is against me. By faith I confess that I am victorious and everything I touch and do will carry the mark of God's blessing.

I am blessed and highly favoured.

DILIGENCE

KEY SCRIPTURE - PROVERBS 21:5A

"The thoughts of the diligent tend only to plenteousness;"

I believe and confess that the Lord is good. He teaches my hand to war and keeps His faithful promises to prosper me. I am anointed to operate in diligence and overcome complacency. Success attends whatever I do. I shall complete everything I start. I take authority over every work of satan and reject his bondage. I am anointed for creativity.

I believe and confess that I am fervent and zealous in the Lord. The grace to pursue and possess the blessing of the Lord operates through me.

I thank the Lord for the ability to endure hardness as a good soldier of Jesus Christ. I rejoice because the word of God keeps me and holds me in the path of righteousness. I boldly declare that I shall not fail or falter for the grace of God helps me to lay my hand on the plough and not to look back.

I boldly break every tendency that wants to drag me back to the old life. I command that every hindrance to

my progress be removed from my way I deliver myself by
faith from every inordinate desires in the name of Jesus. I
refuse every excuse for failure and declare my
commitment to winning. I believe that everything I lay
my hands on prospers. The Lord causes me to go from
victory to victory.

I am blessed and highly favoured.

DIVINE
ACCELERATION

KEY SCRIPTURE - EpHESIANS 3:20

"Now unto him that is able to do exceeding abundantly above all that we ask or think, according to the power that worketh in us,"

I believe and confess that God's divine ability works in my life and causes me to overtake those who have gone ahead. I confess that the anointing to catch up and overtake in all areas or calling is upon my life. The Lord who caused Elijah to outrun chariots shall cause me to accelerate in my victory and blessings.

I confess that like Joseph, I am coming out of the prison of humiliation and limitation into the palaces of promotion and elevation. I believe and confess that my dreams are coming to pass for the Lord will cause others to bless me even as He promotes me.

I confess that my blessings shall be manifest for all to see. The spirit of the Lord rests upon my life and brings transformation. The Lord causes the breakthrough that cancels the pain of the past and blesses my future generation, to come into my life .

I believe and confess that my latter days shall be greater that the former for the Lord will cause a turnaround to the adverse situation I am facing right now. I prophesy divine acceleration to the change I expect in areas of adversity in my life. I speak forth divine restoration to the areas where I have experienced a setback for the Lord Himself will hasten a move that shall overtake all that has put me down and all that has left me behind.

Breakthrough comes into my life and causes the ploughman to overtake the reaper. For the day of the Lord's favour is upon me. My days of harvest are here. My best days are around the corner.

My time of promotion is in hand for the Lord will cause me to possess everything that the enemy stole.

I am blessed and highly favoured.

Divine Elevation

Key Scripture - Psalm 112:9

"He hath dispersed, he hath given to the poor; his righteousness endureth for ever; his horn shall be exalted with honour."

I believe and confess that the favour of the Lord is in my life, the steadfast love of the Lord never fails. He is loving me and lifting me out of the dust of defeat. He has brought me into a place of promotion.

By faith, I confess that the cycle of degradation is broken in my life. For the Lord has made me sit in the heavenly places with Him. My promotion is of the Lord and not from man. I confess boldly that every pit that the enemy has dug for my life will become a stepping stone.

I confess that the prosperity of God rests upon my life. For the Lord makes room for me and increases my capacity. The testimony of the Lord in my life shall be of promotion and operating on a higher dimension. The kind of promotion that will take me from prison to palace comes into my life. I receive divine endorsement.

I believe and confess that the deeper knowledge of the Lord and wisdom from above flows in my life. No temptation shall pull me down, for the Lord Himself promotes me and lifts my hand in the midst of adversity to possess the land.

I confess boldly, that the horn of my strength shall be exalted and the grace of God shall abound in my life for all eyes to see.

I boldly confess that I have come out of sadness into God's rejoicing.

I am blessed and highly favoured.

DIVINE FAVOUR

KEY SCRIPTURE - PROVERbS 12:2A

"A good man obtaineth favour of the LORD:"

I believe and confess that God's plan is to prosper me and not to harm me. God's plan is to elevate me and not to demote me because, eye hath not seen, ear hath not heard nor hath it come into our understanding what God still hath in store for me. The Lord gives me joy in all things, causing favour and blessing to flow towards me. The favour of the Lord goes everywhere with me and the Lord's blessing is manifest even in adverse situations. God's favour to collect the goods from the wicked ones rests upon me. God's divine elevation in the sight of the enemy rests upon my life. The eyes of the Lord go with me and cause me to stand before kings and to have favour with all men.

The favour of the Lord brings notice to my life in the presence of those who will bless and promote me for

God's destined programme will bring favour to my life. I believe and confess that the favour and honour which will frustrate the enemy has rested upon my life. The favour of the Lord which brings me good understanding is coming my way. I am receiving breakthrough ideas which open the doors unto me to help me confront the wrong and be favoured with new understanding. I believe and confess that I will be patient until the day of my promotion.

I confess boldly that the kindness of the Lord upon my life extends to the Heavens. God satisfies my mouth with good things. He took my mourning and gave me laughter, weeping may have been for a night but my joy has come. The favour of God's anointing and strength is upon my life, it flows in me and causes me to rise above all situations. The favour which follows a wise servant is upon my life.

I am blessed and highly favoured.

DIVINE VINDICATION

KEY SCRIPTURE - Isaiah 54:17

"No weapon that is formed against thee shall prosper; and every tongue that shall rise against thee in judgment thou shalt condemn. This is the heritage of the servants of the LORD, and their righteousness is of me, saith the LORD."

I believe and confess that because the Lord will uphold me at all times, I make progress in all that I do. He knows and shall make the counsel of the enemy to be without power. I believe and confess that the Lord shall confound the expectation of the enemy who thinks there is no hope for me.

I boldly confess that the Lord rises on my behalf and breaks the cheekbone of satan. The Lord Himself will bring victory to my circumstance. I shall experience a revelation of the arm of the Lord; for the Lord Himself shall swallow up the spirit of death and promote victory in my life.

I boldly confess the vindication of the Lord which shall result in my harvest of blessings from all battles. I shall increase on all sides. I take my stand against the wiles of the enemy in the name of Jesus.

By faith I confess that I overcome the world in the name of the Lord. Everything that comes against me one way flees seven ways. The weapons of the enemy shall be ineffective over my life. The victory which the Lord brings will silence those who hate me.

Every opposition falls before me for the Lord will strengthen my hand against my strongest enemy. The strategies of the Balaks of this world shall be nullified by the blood of Jesus. The trap of the enemy which was built for me, shall be exposed and destroyed. Every evil counsel of Ahithrophel against me shall not stand. I boldly proclaim my victory and deliverance from sin.

I confess God's assured blessing upon my life. I confess victory over death, victory that brings promotion, victory which puts me above the petty attacks of the enemy, victory that puts me in the heavenly places, victory that applies the blood of Jesus and brings me total vindication.

I am blessed and highly favoured.

DOMINION

KEY SCRIPTURE - PSALM 37:34

"Wait on the LORD, and keep his way, and he shall exalt thee to inherit the land: when the wicked are cut off, thou shalt see it."

I believe and confess that the Lord is good. I give God praise for His victory and dominion over the challenges of life. I thank the Lord because His dominion is an everlasting dominion.

I boldly confess that God causes me to break the evil dominion of the enemy over my life and to exercise the same dominion over everything around me in the name of Jesus.

According to God's word, I will always be above situations. I command that everything that rises against me will remain under my authority in the name of Jesus. Death has no power over me for the Lord who is mightier is in me.

I confess that I will reach my destined position as ordained by the Lord. I believe and confess that the enemy will not triumph over any area of my life. I exercise the authority and dominion which follows the upright in Jesus name.

I boldly declare my dominion from place to place. I have dominion over the challenges that have troubled my mind. I have victory over death regardless of my immediate circumstance. I disallow sickness and disease in my body in the name of Jesus. I exercise dominion over every spirit that tries to break the peace of God in my life and in my home. I thank the Lord for the power to release on earth all that has been granted by Heaven.

I boldly declare that every generational curse that hinders my flow in Christ is nullified in the name of Jesus and I declare that every spirit contrary to the spirit of Christ is under subjection. For God gives me victory, favour and dominion.

I am blessed and highly favoured.

ENCOURAGEMENT

KEY SCRIPTURE - JUDGES 20:22

"And the people the men of Israel encouraged themselves, and set their battle again in array in the place where they put themselves in array the first day."

I believe and confess that the Lord is my portion. He has given me the grace to be strengthened in my inner man. I am encouraged, for the Lord is my source. When I am faced with trials or experience betrayal, the presence of the Lord comforts me. He turns the place of my defeat to my source of victory.

I confess by faith that God will make me an encouragement to the discouraged, a lifter of weakened hand. He fills my mouth with encouraging words and uses me to raise other men for His glory. The word of the Lord proceeds from me to encourage other people's vision, calling and blessing.

I believe and confess that I have victory over discouragement, and I have been anointed to overcome the attacks of satan.

I am blessed and highly favoured.

ENDURANCE

KEY SCRIPTURE - 2 TIMOTHY 2:12

"If we suffer, we shall also reign with him: if we deny him, he also will deny us:"

I believe and confess that the Lord is good. His faithfulness abounds for me at all times. God is my encouragement when I face major and minor problems. What I am going through shall not stop me from where He is taking me. I am free from despair and fear. My eyes are on the Lord and He shall see me through to the end of the matter.

I boldly confess that my steps are ordered of the Lord and He shall lead me to the path of success. The Lord gives me the fruit of patience, and no weapon of satan shall quench the light of God in me.

My eyes are on the Lord the Author and Finisher of my faith. I shall endure until the promise becomes a reality.

I rejoice in the Lord because my weeping may have endured for a night but my joy flows in the morning of life. I boldly declare that the Lord strengthens me and causes me to wait until my change comes.

I confess by faith that even the attacks of the devil on my life and property will not turn around my life. I have started and I shall finish well. I reject and refuse the temptation of compromise. I refuse to bow to circumstance. The name of Jesus and the power of the Holy Spirit is enough for me in every situation for the Lord has promised me that He will never leave me nor forsake me.

I am blessed and highly favoured.

EXAMPLE

KEY SCRIPTURE - 1 PETER 2:21

"For even hereunto were ye called: because Christ also suffered for us, leaving us an example, that ye should follow his steps:"

I believe and confess that the Lord is good. His faithfulness is forever. The Lord has called me to be a testimony of His power. He has endued me with the spirit of a servant to serve like Jesus did. My life shall be a challenge to those who observe me. The words that proceed from me will build other people.

I boldly confess that I am an example of God's blessing, favour and goodness. I manifest the transformation which the Holy Spirit brings.

I receive the grace to overcome persecution and refuse to take vengeance and be an able witness of Jesus Christ.

I believe and confess that Gods grace strengthens me to be an example to the believer. Everyday he helps me so His words proceed from my mouth to build other in the faith. I believe and confess that I receive the grace to challenge others to live a life that glorifies God. I thank the Lord for the privilege to be counted worthy to be called His child. I give God praise for helping me to observe and to live a life that bring a testimony to His holy name.

I am blessed and highly favoured.

FAITH

KEY SCRIPTURE - HEBREWS 11:6

"But without faith it is impossible to please him: for he that cometh to God must believe that he is, and that he is a rewarder of them that diligently seek him."

I thank the Lord for causing me to have victory through the Lord Jesus Christ.

I boldly declare that I am filled with the God kind of faith. The faith of God in me strengthens me to speak to the mountains of challenges. The mountains bow to the word of God. My hope comes to pass. My vision is realised.

By faith I come against situations and circumstances and gain control through the Lord Jesus Christ. Fear is not my portion. Traditions of man shall not control me. Satan and his demons have no control over me for I am filled with the faith that overcomes the world.

Through faith I speak to every satanic manifestation and produce financial and spiritual prosperity.

I confess that I shall enjoy the blessings of a faithful man and obtain a good report through the exercise of my faith.

I am blessed and highly favoured.

FAITHFULNESS OF

GOD

KEY SCRIPTURE - PSALM 36:5

"Thy mercy, O LORD, is in the heavens; and thy faithfulness reacheth unto the clouds."

I believe and confess that the Lord is good. I thank the Lord for His faithfulness at all times in my life. The faithfulness of the Lord is known to me as I face the challenges of life. God will not fail me. He is a covenant keeping God.

His faithfulness makes guidance available in the darkness of this world. His faithfulness will make Him finish what He started in my life. The Lord is more than enough for me, and I trust Him even on to the ends of the earth.

I thank the Lord for He is faithful for He has started a good work in me and He will finish it. The Lord Himself shall make me to experience His blessing on a day by day basis. I praise the name of the Lord because He is a covenant keeping God. His word will never fail and He will stand by what He said. Every attempt of the enemy to belittle the goodness of God in my life will be negated by the blood of Jesus. I praise God for His loving kindness and mercy which preserves me in the presence of my enemies. None of His word will go unfulfilled. God's word concerning my destiny is already settled in Heaven.

I am blessed and highly favoured.

FAMILY

KEY SCRIPTURE - EphESIANS 3:14 -15

"For this cause I bow my knees unto the Father of our Lord Jesus Christ,

Of whom the whole family in heaven and earth is named,"

I believe and confess that God is good. I thank the Lord for His faithfulness in my family. I receive the grace of God to maintain unity and love in my marriage.

No weapon formed against my home shall stand, and every mouth that rise against me in judgement, shall be condemned. Every demon against marriage is commanded to leave my home. The spirit of jealousy is bound from coming near my home. My children are covered with the blood of Jesus. My home shall be a place of divine order.

I give God glory because He began a good work in my home and He shall complete it.

By faith I speak the blessings of the Lord on all my children and the future generations. I declare that God has given me a godly family and a godly marriage where there is satisfaction and joy at all times. I receive healing for every heavy handedness with which my parents handled me. I break and cancel the evil consequence of all previous sexual and sinful entanglements.

I boldly declare that the blessings of the Lord flows in my marriage and in my life. The joy of a Christian family abounds. Every programme of satan against my children and my teenage children shall not stand. Mountains of financial problem that have risen against my family shall crumble in the name of the Lord. Generational blessings abounds in my family. Favour and generational grace abounds in my family. I thank the Lord for the wonderful family He has given me according to His promise.

I am blessed and highly favoured.

FEAR

KEY SCRIPTURE - 2 TIMOTHY 1:7

"For God hath not given us the spirit of fear; but of power, and of love, and of a sound mind."

I believe and confess that I have victory over the challenges of life, for the Lord has promised not to leave or forsake me. I receive boldness instead of fear to face the challenges.

I boldly declare that the weapons of the enemy shall have no effect on me. I reject the interference of the spirit of fear, the fear of the future, the fear of failure, the fear of success, and all other fears. I break every tormenting effect which fear has had over my life, and I declare that all news contrary to my joy shall be turned around. I receive the heart of a Godly fear to honour and magnify the Lord, and not the problems. I receive God's grace to trust Him without doubt.

I thank the Lord for giving me victory over the challenges of life. I rejoice in Him for He has promised not to leave me nor forsake me. I praise him because according to Him, the weapons of the enemy shall not overcome me. I give God praise because He has commanded His dread to be in the heart of those who have risen against me. I rejoice by faith in anticipation of God turning every news contrary to my joy around. I boldly declare that I am free from the fear of people. Fear shall not control me. I am filled with faith. I thank the Lord for filling my heart only with godly fear.

I am blessed and highly favoured.

FINANCE

Key Scripture - Deuteronomy 8:18

*"But thou shalt remember the LORD thy God: for it is
he that giveth thee power to get wealth, that he may
establish his covenant which he sware unto thy fathers,
as it is this day."*

I believe and confess that the Lord is good. He is
faithful to all those who trust in Him.

I give God praise for His increase in my life and the
blessing which He has brought. I rejoice because the
Lord has brought in my life the blessing that maketh rich.
He has given me the seed of finance to minister to others,
who lack. This is my day of bumper harvest. This is my
time of increase in everything I do. The storehouse is full
with God's abundance.

Through God I declare my freedom from the
shackles of debt. I worship the Lord who owns the cattle
upon a thousand hills. I give Him praise for making me a
partaker of the wealth of the wicked. I am financially
buoyant in Christ, enjoying His increase everyday.

I give God praise because He is my channel of
blessing therefore He has broken the yoke of poverty over

my family. He has established me as a wealth producer.
By faith I receive the blessings that makes rich. I give
God praise because the seed of finance to minister to
other people increases in my life. I believe and confess
that the Holy Spirit makes my heart tender towards seed
sowing. He causes me to be a promoter of the work of
the Kingdom therefore I confess that I receive increase in
the name of Jesus. Everything I touch abounds with the
riches of Christ. My land, my home and my work is
covered with the favour of the Lord. I have been called to
create wealth and I shall flow in my calling.

I am blessed and highly favoured.

Focus

Key Scripture - Hebrews 12:2

"Looking unto Jesus the author and finisher of our faith; who for the joy that was set before him endured the cross, despising the shame, and is set down at the right hand of the throne of God."

I give God praise for the wondrous work He is doing in my life. I thank God because He is the Author and Finisher of my faith.

I reject every form of satanic destruction and break free from them. My life is anointed to carry out the programme of God. Therefore, I reject every time wasting dream, and every tendency of jealousy over other people's gifts.

The grace of the Lord abounds to me and opens me to the abilities deposited in me. I shall possess my possession and see the fulfilment of my vision. My eyes are on the breakthrough despite contrary report. I break free from ungodly habits that are holding me back.

I confess that I shall become a meaningful achiever in the specific area of my calling.

I am blessed and highly favoured.

FORGIVENESS

Key Scripture - Ephesians 4:32

"And be ye kind one to another, tenderhearted, forgiving one another, even as God for Christ's sake hath forgiven you."

I believe and confess that the Lord is good and His mercy endures forever. The Lord has changed my mourning into dancing again, for He has cleansed me from all unrighteousness and sin.

I believe and confess that the riches of God's grace abound to me and helps me to forgive those who have offended me.

God fills me with unconditional love and I refuse to live in offence against other people. I choose to bless and not to curse. I have found that I have the ability to live in peace, for I am filled with the love of God. The Lord has redeemed my life from destruction and set my feet on the solid rock.

I give God praise for taking care of my past and guaranteeing my future. The Lord has forgiven all my sins and cleansed me from all unrighteousness therefore, I release all those who have offended me I thank the Lord for the grace to reach out in love to those who have violated me. I give God praise because I shall not hold anyone in unforgiveness. By faith I stand under the blood and plead the blood against every unforgiving spirit. I receive the grace to walk in forgiveness and to heal other peoples pains. I thank the Lord for redeeming my life from destruction in Jesus name.

I am blessed and highly favoured.

FREEDOM FROM BONDAGE

KEY SCRIPTURE - ObadiaH 1:17

"But upon mount Zion shall be deliverance, and there shall be holiness; and the house of Jacob shall possess their possessions."

I give God praise for freedom, which He has given me in the Holy Spirit. I thank the Lord for He had made me totally victorious over every binding spirit. In the name of the Lord Jesus, I am free from the bondage of depression, I am free from the tendency of a spirit of desperation and my heart is free from a fault-finding spirit.

I am filled with the spirit of boldness. I overcome every tendency that is contrary to the presence of the Holy Spirit. I am a child of God and God gives me victory over every doubtful spirit, unhealthy competition and the tendency to be blindly aggressive.

I confess by faith that the blood of Jesus works in

my life against every seductive spirit and sets me totally free from every tendency of the enemy.

I confess that I am free from the spirit of unhappiness and depression. The spirit of the Lord breaks me free from the feeling of worthlessness. I am free from every tendency of being unstable. By faith, I confess that the Holy Spirit has given me victory in every area of my life and I am growing in the grace of Jesus Christ, overcoming daily by the spirits word. I am not a slave any more to any bondage but totally free in Jesus Christ.

I am blessed and highly favoured.

FRUITFULNESS

KEY SCRIPTURE - GENESIS 1:28

"And God blessed them, and God said unto them, Be fruitful, and multiply, and replenish the earth, and subdue it: and have dominion over the fish of the sea, and over the fowl of the air, and over every living thing that moveth upon the earth."

I believe and confess that the Lord is good, He causes me to have victory at all times. Through Him, fruitfulness follows everything I do. I am the planting of the Lord and fruitfulness follows me wherever I am. The grace of the Lord delivers me from spiritual barrenness, God brings fruitfulness in every area where there has been barrenness in my life in the name of Jesus.

I boldly confess, that increase follows everything I do. In old age I shall still bear fruit that brings glory to God. I shall bear the fruit of patience in my life in the name of Jesus. By faith, I command that every barrenness in my life will break forth with fruitfulness. I shall see my children's children and blessings in all that I do. The Lord will turn the place of my enslavement to be the place of fruitfulness. The Lord will transform my life from one degree of fruitfulness to a greater one.

I confess the blessings of the Lord on the labour of my hand, I declare that I am a partaker of the initiatives I am involved in and in my trying times, fruit will follow my effort. I shall have reasons to praise God at all times for I shall see the fruit of my lips created.

I am blessed and highly favoured.

FUTURE

Key Scripture - Philippians 3:14

"I press toward the mark for the prize of the high calling of God in Christ Jesus."

I bless the name of the Lord for His daily leading. I thank Him for not withholding any good thing from me, because I trust Him.

I boldly confess that all things will work together for my good, because I love the Lord. The future of my marriage is secure in the Lord. The future of my children is secure in the Lord. My future will portray God's manifest blessing.

I boldly confess that the Lord is my Shepherd, therefore, I shall not miss my purpose, for the Lord has built His hedge around me to give me protection and guarantees my future. Everything I lay my hand on shall be accomplished, for the Lord will cause success to attend all that I do.

The Lord destroys every impending trouble that rises against me. He causes me to forget all my past achievements and to reach forth to the challenges ahead.

I confess that God advances me and helps me to finish my race with joy. The Lord will lead me for He has begun a good work in me and shall help me until the end. By faith I thank the Lord for the promise not to withhold good things from me therefore, by faith I commit every of my work into His hands and I rejoice because the coming years shall bring forth His blessings and His glory. I refuse every excessive weight of distraction which the enemy may want to use against my future. I reject ever negative confession that has been made into my life in the past. I thank the Lord in advance for the hedge He has already built into my future.

I am blessed and highly favoured.

GLORY

KEY SCRIPTURE - HAGGAI 2:9

"The glory of this latter house shall be greater than of the former, saith the LORD of hosts: and in this place will I give peace, saith the LORD of hosts."

I believe and confess that the Lord is good. His glorious presence is manifest in my life.

I boldly confess that the earth is filled with His glory. I thank the Lord for the privilege of manifesting His glory on earth. Jesus reigns in my life and in everything I do. My ministry will bring glory, for through me He shall heal the sick, destroy bondage and set captives free. His glory fills our church.

The glory of the Lord shall be manifest in our church, in our city, and in our days.

I rejoice in the Lord because the glory of the Lord shall be released everywhere I am for his glory shall invade my chaos and emptiness and turn it into pleasantness. I give God praise because He brings His presence into my life and transforms my desert into a land of fruitfulness for the Glory of the Lord shall be revealed in my life and all eyes shall see it. His glory shall be released in my Church, it shall be released in my home and it shall be released in my work and the glory of the Lord that shines forth from my life shall be for healing of the nations. I boldly declare that the Lord will manifest His splendour through my life. I thank the Lord for creating me to pleasure Him with praise. I give God praise for sparking the fire of revival in my heart and I rejoice in the Lord for the joy unspeakable and full of His glory.

I am blessed and highly favoured.

GROWTH

KEY SCRIPTURE - PSALM 92:12

"The righteous shall flourish like the palm tree: he shall grow like a cedar in Lebanon."

I believe and confess that the Lord is good. Every word of the Lord in my life shall bring forth fruit.

I boldly declare that I have received grace to grow in my relationship with Him. The seed of God's Word will fall on good soil in my life.

By faith I confess that I have received grace to walk with God and to understand His Word. His Word bears fruit in my life, for the success of the Lord attends all I do.

I boldly declare that I receive grace to put away immature behaviour and to grow more in the Lord. My eyes are open to the deeper things of God. I am increasing in the knowledge of the Lord. I soar above all situations like an eagle. I am experiencing an all round growth.

I am blessed and highly favoured.

GUIDANCE

KEY SCRIPTURE - PSALM 78:72

*"So he fed them according to the integrity of his heart;
and guided them by the skilfulness of his hands."*

I believe and confess that the Lord is good. I rejoice before Him with gratefulness for His daily leading. The Spirit of the Lord is my guide through the darkness of this world. He orders my steps so that I do not fear.

I boldly confess that my confidence is in the Lord and not an earthly guide. He leads me and shows me the way. The hand of the Lord shall lead me in my career. My steps are ordered to the place of fruitfulness. I receive the anointing of the Holy Spirit for every endeavour I embark on. He will lead me to accomplish what I began.

I thank the Lord for ordering my steps. I rejoice in Him because He helps me so that I will not be led astray. I give God praise because the Holy Spirit is my friend and my guide in the darkness of this world. I boldly declare that the Lord Himself shall see me through the valleys and the mountains and every step I take shall bring glory to His name. My steps shall be ordered by the Lord; for the Lord Himself will give me clear direction in everything I do. I rejoice in the Lord because He exposes every danger ahead and He makes me to ride upon the high places. By faith, I declare that the Lord upholds me in the right way so that I do not go astray.

I confess that I shall hear His voice at every cross road as he leads me in the path I should go. I bless God because every Red Sea of impossible situation is turning around for my favour and my good. The Lord will guide me continually until I see Him face to face.

I am blessed and highly favoured.

HEALING

KEY SCRIPTURE - Exodus 15:26

"And said, If thou wilt diligently hearken to the voice of the LORD thy God, and wilt do that which is right in his sight, and wilt give ear to his commandments, and keep all his statutes, I will put none of these diseases upon thee, which I have brought upon the Egyptians: for I am the LORD that healeth thee."

I believe and confess that the Lord is good. He is faithful at all times to keep His Word. God will not withhold good things from those who love Him. I give praise to the Lord for His work of healing in my life.

I take authority over every affliction and destroy the impact of sickness. I command diseases in the bone to die. I curse every impurity of the blood. I take authority over every disease of the heart and receive healing, in the name of Jesus. Cancer and other destructive diseases have no power over me, for the Lord God is my Jehovah Rapha. He remembers my tears of affliction and takes away tears from members of my household.

I believe and confess that I have inner healing for ailments I cannot see. Every satanic virus is cursed to the root. Affliction is not my portion. I reject every problem of blood disease and receive healing for every area of my life.

I boldly confess that I am anointed to bring healing to the masses of the people. The Lord shall deliver those in bondage through me. The ministry of healing shall flow forth through me, in the Name of Jesus.

I am blessed and highly favoured.

HONOUR

Key Scripture - 1 Peter 2:9

"But ye are a chosen generation, a royal priesthood, an holy nation, a peculiar people; that ye should shew forth the praises of him who hath called you out of darkness into his marvellous light:"

I believe and confess that the Lord is good. His faithfulness is forever.

I confess that I am clothed with honour and glory and called to bring honour to the name of the Lord.

I boldly confess that the riches of God and the favour of the Lord is reserved for the righteous and flowing to me. Everything I am and everything I have honours the Lord. My heart is teachable and ready to receive His honour.

I thank Him for teaching my heart to walk after His counsel on a day by day basis. The Lord will make me to be clothed with His honour and glory. I rejoice in the Lord because He opens my eyes to the various ways that I can bring honour to His holy name. I receive honour, riches and favour from the Lord as a blessing which He has reserved for His own righteous ones. I make a commitment to always honour the prophets of God and to receive their reward in Jesus name.

I boldly declare that all the glory that belongs to God shall always go to Him. All the honour that is His shall flow forth from my mouth and I shall lift up the Lord at all times. I rejoice for the Lord has given me victory and has lifted me over the enemy.

I am blessed and highly favoured.

HUNGER FOR RIGHTEOUSNESS

KEY SCRIPTURE - MATTHEW 5:6

"Blessed are they which do hunger and thirst after righteousness: for they shall be filled."

I believe and confess that the grace of God is sufficient for me. I have been delivered from the power and penalty of sin.

I boldly declare that everything I am and have is for the kingdom of God. My heart is yielded to do the will of God. His love fills my heart. I am anointed to operate in holy zeal.

I boldly declare that the grace of God shall help me to be faithful to the end, to walk in righteousness in my inner life, and my life shall be a mirror of His grace.

I receive boldness to break free from bondage, to endure persecutions and be wise in my associations.

I boldly declare that the voice of the Holy Spirit will lead me and my hunger after His purpose shall increase.

I am blessed and highly favoured.

IMPOSSIBILITY

Key Scripture - Luke 1:37

"For with God nothing shall be impossible."

I bless the Name of the Lord for proving Himself mighty and strong in my life. I praise Him for His promise not to withhold any good thing from me.

I boldly declare He is in charge for all that concerns me. The mountain of impossibility turns around to breakthrough, in the Name of Jesus.

I thank the Lord for counting me worthy to face the challenge before me. I praise Him because it shall result in my promotion.

I boldly confess that my miracle will become a reality, for the Lord will supply that which seems impossible. The ocean I see before me today will turn around to a miracle. I shall be victorious over the wild attacks of satan.

I am blessed and highly favoured.

INCREASE

KEY SCRIPTURE - DEUTERONOMY 7:13

*"And he will love thee, and bless thee, and multiply thee:
he will also bless the fruit of thy womb, and the fruit of
thy land, thy corn, and thy wine, and thine oil, the
increase of thy kine, and the flocks of thy sheep, in the
land which he sware unto thy fathers to give thee."*

I believe and confess that the Lord is faithful at all
times. I praise Him for causing me to experience increase
with Him and with man.

I boldly confess that my eyes are anointed to
discover and enjoy the favour of the Lord.

I boldly confess the favour of God on my business and
everything I lay my hands on. Supernatural breakthrough
follows me. I am experiencing God's abundant increase. I
am anointed to experience multiple increase. Barrenness is
over, in Jesus Name. I shall increase in spiritual
understanding. There shall be exceedingly great increase
in blessing, and favour. The days of my small beginnings
will turn around to the time of great abundance.

I believe and confess that I am increasing in the
statue and knowledge of the fullness of Christ. By faith, I

grow daily and bring forth fruit to the glory of God. For the Lord Himself helps me and causes me to increase in the fruit of righteousness. I give God praise for making this a year of increase and favour.

I am blessed and highly favoured.

INSECURITY

KEY SCRIPTURE - PSALM 56:11

"In God have I put my trust: I will not be afraid what man can do unto me."

I believe and confess that the Lord is faithful at all times and rejoice in Him for good and His life at the cross at Calvary.

I boldly confess that the Lord is breaking the impact of negative upbringing and negative relationships in my life. I receive God's freedom from every tendency of blaming others. I reject the spirit of the fear of man, for the Lord has given me the Spirit of love, boldness and a sound mind. I am free from unforgiveness. I am free from self-rejection. The negatives of the past shall not stop the blessings in my future.

I believe and confess that the love of the Lord increases in my life and the favour of God is upon my life. I am free from every for of insecurity for the Lord has broken the impact of every negativity impacted into me from childhood and He has set me free from the bondage of insecurity. Everyday, I find a new identity and personhood in the Holy Ghost. My life is full of the grace of God and I am an extension of the kingdom of Jesus. I believe and confess that I am released from every bondage and every disease that has come through unforgiveness. I am free from the spirit of selfishness and every self-centred behaviour. I am a new man in Christ. I am secure in the Lord.

I am blessed and highly favoured.

JOY

KEY SCRIPTURE - ISAIAH 29:19

*"The meek also shall increase their joy in the LORD,
and the poor among men shall rejoice in the Holy One
Of Israel."*

I believe and confess that the Lord is good. He fills
me with joy unspeakable and full of glory. The Lord has
given me a reason to celebrate, for He has filled my
mouth with laughter.

I boldly confess that the shout of joy will be heard in
my dwelling. The breakthrough of God's supply will
come into my life.

By faith I speak to every situation that I am facing and
confess that I will experience the favour that will be
manifest to all men.

God has began a good thing in my life and He will
surely perfect it. My prayers will be answered. My heart
will be continually filled with His joy, I shall not eat the
bread of sorrow.

My mourning will change to joy and the song of joy
shall not cease in my house.

I am blessed and highly favoured.

KEEPING ON

KEY SCRIPTURE - JAMES 1:12

"Blessed is the man that endureth temptation: for when he is tried, he shall receive the crown of life, which the Lord hath promised to them that love him."

I give praise to the Name of the Lord, because He has always caused me to know His victory. God who began a good work in me shall complete it.

I boldly confess my victory over discouragement and every lie of satan. Through the Lord I shall endure every tough time, and come out victorious. My fiery trials will result in boldness and strength.

I boldly confess that every trouble I face will only reveal the light of God in me. When I pass through the fire I shall not be put to shame. I receive grace to stand until my change comes, for the Lord will turn my tears to joy.

I rejoice in the Lord because nothing shall cause me to cease remaining in the love of God. By faith, my anchor holds firm in the midst of rolling billows, reproach and persecution, the power of God shall be manifest in my life. I give God praise for causing His grace to be sufficient for me. I abound unto all good works and receive the ability to stand when the going is tough. I believe and confess that the Lord is perfecting, establishing and strengthening me at all times.

I am blessed and highly favoured.

KNOWLEDGE

KEY SCRIPTURE - PROVERBS 1:7

"The fear of the LORD is the beginning of knowledge: but fools despise wisdom and instruction."

I believe and confess that I have a heart that desires the knowledge of God. The knowledge of the Lord is pleasant to my soul, and causes me to increase in everything I do. I receive the ability to flow in divine knowledge.

I confess that I have insight from God into peoples real problem. The knowledge of the Lord helps me to bring solution to their lives. I am a blessing, to my generation.

I boldly confess that through me words of excellence and wisdom will flow. The words that proceed from me will bless those who come in contact with me.

I believe and confess that I have received the anointing to operate in supernatural knowledge. The treasures of wisdom and knowledge are residing in me. Through God, I have the grace to walk in His wisdom.

I am blessed and highly favoured.

LABOUR

Key Scripture - Ecclesiastes 5:19

"Every man also to whom God hath given riches and wealth, and hath given him power to eat thereof, and to take his portion, and to rejoice in his labour; this is the gift of God."

I believe and confess that the grace of the Lord is sufficient for me for all occasions. I thank the Lord for the covenant of His blessing on the labour of my hand.

I boldly declare that the blessing of the Lord rest upon that which I do. I confess that I shall walk in wisdom and prudence to manage what God has provided. I reject every influence of the devourer and the destroyer. I reject the tendency of laziness and burn out.

I confess, by faith, that the labour of my hands shall not fail, and in the day of my harvest I shall not bring forth for trouble, nor reap adversity. The Lord will cause a period of harvest to follow the season of my labour.

I am blessed and highly favoured.

LOVE

KEY SCRIPTURE - 1 JOHN 4:7

"Beloved, let us love one another: for love is of God; and every one that loveth is born of God, and knoweth God."

I give God the praise for His love and kindness which He shows me daily. I thank the Lord for His Spirit that imparts and sheds the love of God in my heart.

I boldly confess that in Christ Jesus I am able to walk in Godly love. The love of the Lord which flows from my heart will bring healing to other people.

I boldly confess that the fruit of God's love is manifest through me. I have received the Spirit of love in place of fear.

By faith I declare my freedom from hypocrisy and will also confess that I increase daily in the love of God. My life shall be a mirror of the God kind of love.

I believe and confess that the grace to continue in the love of God resides in me. It helps me and breaks the power of that which is trying to separate me from the love of God. I rejoice in the Lord for He fills me with the fruit of love. I choose to walk in the grace of the Lord and not in unforgiveness. I give God praise for His marvellous love that sought for me and brought me out of darkness. I boldly confess that my life is crowned with God's loving kindness and mercy.

I am blessed and highly favoured.

OBEDIENCE

KEY SCRIPTURE - ISAIAH 1:19

"If ye be willing and obedient, ye shall eat the good of the land:"

I believe and confess that the Lord is good. His faithfulness extends to the generations. The Lord is my strength and He enables me to walk in humility and transparency of heart. No evil contamination comes into my heart, in Jesus Name.

I believe and confess that I have received the grace of God to walk in obedience and unlock His blessings. Through God I shall not fail or fall. His mighty hand upholds me. He gives me strength to walk in the light and makes my feet like hinds feet. I am willing and obedient, I will eat the best of the land.

I believe and confess that I receive grace to walk in obedience and it will unlock my breakthrough. I thank the Lord because He will cause me to succeed as I do His will. By faith, I receive the ability to do that which pleasures God. I believe and confess that every thought that exalts itself above the knowledge of Christ in my life is brought to nought.

I am blessed and highly favoured.

OPPRESSION

KEY SCRIPTURE - DEUTERONOMY 26:7

*"And when we cried unto the LORD God of our fathers,
the LORD heard our voice, and looked on our affliction,
and our labour, and our oppression:"*

I thank the Lord because He causes me to have victory at all times. The Word of God puts me over situations and circumstances, greater is He that is in me than He that is in the world.

I take authority over satanic operation. The Name of the Lord is my refuge and therefore the operation of the enemy is broken. The operation of poverty, sickness and disease loses its grip over my life.

I believe and confess that the Lord makes me His instrument of healing to broken people. I give thanks to Him for making the programme of the oppressor to fail.

I am blessed and highly favoured.

OVERCOMING WEARINESS

KEY SCRIPTURE - MATTHEW 11:28

"Come unto me, all ye that labour and are heavy laden, and I will give you rest."

I believe and confess that I overcome weariness. I thank the Lord for being a covenant keeping God. I bless His name for His faithfulness which extends to the heavens.

By faith I confess that the Lord becomes my rock in a weary land and helps me to overcome and to stand in Jesus name. I confess that my weakness becomes my source of strength through the Lord Jesus and in my moments of tiredness, He shall increase my might. I receive strength to carry out my ministry and to experience a harvest of blessing.

I believe and confess that the Lord will use me to sow the seed of favour in other people's life and help me not to be lukewarm but zealous for His kingdom. The

Lord will cause mercy to flow in my life to touch hurting people.

I believe and confess that my tears of weariness becomes my song of victory. The Lord, Himself, shall break the power of the enemy and God will give me a reason to praise Him as He supplies strength in the time of trouble.

I believe and confess that I have overcome weariness while studying the word of God and I have received boldness and a new craving for God's word. My eyes are open to see and to minister to those who are weary. I boldly declare that the burden removing, yoke destroying power of God rests upon my life. I go from weariness to total victory.

I am blessed and Highly favoured.

PEACE

KEY SCRIPTURE - PhilippiANS 4:7

*"And the peace of God, which passeth all understanding,
shall keep your hearts and minds through Christ Jesus."*

I give praise to the Lord for His unspeakable joy and
peace which floods my life. God is faithful, He keeps in
perfect peace those whose mind is rested on Him. The
peace of God that passes understanding surrounds me.
Therefore, I am not afraid.

I receive the peace of God for every step I take. I am
free from anxiety and increase in the peace of God that is
like a river. The Lord will cause His peace to increase in
my habitation.

I believe and confess that the peace that passes
understanding keeps and garrisons my heart. I confess by
faith that I walk and operate under the covering and
canopy of God's peace. The peace of God is released
upon my household. The peace of God is released
around my dwelling place. No danger befalls me. No
trouble comes near me. I give God praise for His peace
and safety of the night.

I take authority over the spirit of anxiety and break its hold over my life. I rejoice in the Lord for guiding my future with His peace. I prophesy peace that flows like a river into my destiny.

I am blessed and highly favoured.

PERSEVERANCE

KEY SCRIPTURE - JAMES 5:11

"Behold, we count them happy which endure. Ye have heard of the patience of Job, and have seen the end of the Lord; that the Lord is very pitiful, and of tender mercy."

I give praise to the Lord for His faithfulness and grace in the face of challenges. I thank the Lord for His strength which upholds me.

I believe and confess that I can do all things through Christ Who strengthens me. No mountain of impossibility shall stop me, for the Lord will turn every attack to a testimony. Every fiery dart of the enemy shall be ineffective, for the eyes of the Lord are upon me for good.

I come against every dart of the enemy which he uses against me. I take authority over the power of satan and destroy every weapon. I confess that the hold of discouragement is broken, for the Lord causes me to operate in His purpose. I believe and confess that nothing should pull me away from spiritual progress for the Lord sets me in motion for promotion and maturity. I shall reach my goal. I shall accomplish my purpose. I shall reach my destiny and climb to a higher dimension.

I am blessed and highly favoured.

PERSISTENCE

KEY SCRIPTURE - JOSHUA 1:6

*"Be strong and of a good courage: for unto this people
shalt thou divide for an inheritance the land, which I
sware unto their fathers to give them."*

I give thanks to the Lord who causes me to have
victory at all times. I bless His Name for the boldness to
stand in the face of great adversity. Through God I will
wait until my change comes. He strengthens me to
succeed where others fail. No wind of opposition shall
draw me back, for the Lord will paralyse every demon
that resists my progress.

I give thanks to the Lord for the patience to inherit
the promise He has made. I thank the Lord in advance
for rewarding my faith.

I believe and confess that in the face of adversity, I
receive strength to stand. I rejoice in Lord because He
has given me grace to manifest breakthrough in my life. I
thank the Lord for helping me to endure as a good soldier
of Jesus Christ. I rejoice in advance for the reward of my
faith.

I am blessed and highly favoured.

POWER

KEY SCRIPTURE - ACTS 1:8

"But ye shall receive power, after that the Holy Ghost is come upon you: and ye shall be witnesses unto me both in Jerusalem, and in all Judaea, and in Samaria, and unto the uttermost part of the earth."

I believe and confess that the Lord is good, and His abilities are residing in me. God's dynamic power is working within me. He has given me the power over all things. Through Him I shall heal the sick, bring deliverance and stop the attack of the enemy.

I believe and confess that the power of God sets me in motion to succeed and not to fail. The Holy Spirit overshadows me and covers me with His anointing.

I believe and confess that the power of God to tread upon serpents, tear down the stronghold of satan, and break down the control of demonic spirits, operate through me. The greater one is in me, and He puts me over and above situations and circumstances.

I am blessed and highly favoured.

PROSPERITY

Key Scripture - 3 John 1:2

"Beloved, I wish above all things that thou mayest prosper and be in health, even as thy soul prospereth."

I believe and confess that the Lord is good. I thank the Lord for causing me to prevail against the programme of the enemy. The Lord gives me grace to sow seed and reap a harvest. It is God's divine pleasure to prosper me.

I receive God's favour and grace to achieve His purpose. I will prosper in all my ways. The Lord will cause me to receive my destined blessing. My life is open to all round prosperity, spirit, soul and body. I receive grace to be a promoter of God's kingdom. I shall be a blessing and a source of strength to the discouraged. Every seed I sow will bring forth the fruit of God's favour. The goodness of the Lord shall not cease in my assembly.

I am blessed and highly favoured.

PRUDENCE

KEY SCRIPTURE - PROVERbs 14:18

"The simple inherit folly: but the prudent are crowned with knowledge."

I believe and confess that the Lord is good. I thank the Lord for His abounding wisdom which flows from Him to His own. I thank the Lord because He causes me to increase in the knowledge of His. God's wisdom makes me a champion over satanic provocation. God's wisdom lifts me above emotional bondage and gives me the grace to overcome every opposition. My steps are ordered of the Lord. My heart is tender to receive His correction.

I believe and confess that I receive understanding to operate in godly prudence. I believe and confess that I have God's ability to walk in love and knowledge. The wisdom of God dwells in me. The ability of God to have insight into situations that are hidden from the worldly wise are made available to me. I am growing daily in the grace of Jesus Christ. I give God the praise for the spirit of discretion, wisdom and understanding.

I am blessed and highly favoured.

PULLING DOWN STRONGHOLDS

KEY SCRIPTURE - JEREMIAH 1:10

"See, I have this day set thee over the nations and over the kingdoms, to root out, and to pull down, and to destroy, and to throw down, to build, and to plant."

I believe and confess that the name of the Lord is my source of constant victory. Every satanic opposition which comes against me is frustrated in the name of the Lord. Every attempt of the enemy to pervert the word of God in my life is nullified in the name of Jesus. For the Lord causes me to be free from every satanic activity. The Lord gives me freedom from the stronghold of the enemy.

I believe and confess that the battles of satan against the life of my family and friends are nullified in the name of Jesus. I uproot every seed of discord which the enemy is sowing in my life, in my work and in my church. The evil seed sown by the enemy shall not rise. I speak boldly against every seducing spirit and I declare my victory over them. I reject every attempt of the enemy to draw me into his lies. I cancel and nullify the spirit of worry and doubt sent to torment my mind.

By faith, I untie the cords of satan that have been woven around people who come my way. I loose them in the name of Jesus. I cast out the spirit of deception that tries to work on me, that tries to lure me away from the purpose and plan of God. I cast down every imagination and every lie that comes from the pit of hell. Every demonic squatter sent around my life is dispersed and destroyed in the name of Jesus. The hold of the spirit of lunacy, palsy, depression and every evil is commanded to be loosed in the name of Jesus.

I boldly confess that the Lord is turning every blow and buffeting of satan to a blessing. God is casting down every lie the enemy is trying to sell to my mind in the name of Jesus. I exercise my legal right as revealed in the word against every weapon of satan. I come against the enemy in the name of Jesus and declare my total victory.

I boldly confess that no weapon of the enemy is effective against me. The power of the in-dwelling spirit of God rises against every lie of the enemy. By faith, I thank the Lord for the redemptive and protective power in the blood of Jesus and therefore declare that every stronghold of the enemy comes down.

I am blessed and highly favoured.

PURPOSE

KEY SCRIPTURE - ROMANS 8:28

"And we know that all things work together for good to them that love God, to them who are the called according to his purpose."

I believe and confess that the purpose of God for my life will stand.

I boldly confess that the Lord causes me to have a future and hope. Therefore, I refuse to be stopped by negative attitude or past achievements.

I boldly confess that my eyes are on my destination and not the success of the past. My vision will come to pass. God gives me the strength to achieve all my goals. When faced with a storm I refuse to bow, but hold on to God's purpose and calling.

I boldly confess that in God's season and timing for my life, the favour of the Lord which He sets in motion, shall come to pass.

I am blessed and highly favoured.

Rest

Key Scripture - Matthew 11:28

"Come unto me, all ye that labour and are heavy laden, and I will give you rest."

I believe and confess that according to the Word of God, I have God's peace that passes understanding. God has broken the hold of the spirit of worry over my life. I shall not be led by what I see, but by the Spirit of the Lord.

By faith I receive grace to rest and trust that God will bring His promises to pass. The Lord is my Shepherd. He leads me beside green pastures. I have His rest I shall not go astray. For the Lord shall be my rest in a weary land.

I believe and confess that the peace of the Holy Spirit increases in my life. The Lord is putting the cohorts of the enemy to flight. I rejoice in the Lord for He has destroyed every trouble and impending danger. I take authority and command everything attached to my destiny, which has been held captive by the enemy, to be broken loose. I rejoice in the rest of God. I meditate on the goodness of God. I glory and recount the bountiful things He has done in my life. I confess that no matter what I go through that the peace of God is enough for me.

I am blessed and highly favoured.

RESTORATION

Key Scripture - Psalm 23:3

"He restoreth my soul: he leadeth me in the paths of righteousness for his name's sake."

I give praise to the Lord for His faithfulness and grace. I thank the Lord for His promise that He will not withhold any good from those who trust Him. God's blessing and favour is restored to me. I receive restoration and help in the place of my brokenness.

I take back every property of mine stolen by the enemy, I reclaim everything which belongs to me.

I believe and confess that principalities and powers are broken on my behalf. The Lord leads me in paths of righteousness and restores my soul. The place of my captivity becomes the house of my restoration.

I believe and confess that the Lord is restoring unto me all that the enemy stole. I take back every property of mine which was stolen by satan. I take back everything hidden from me by the enemy in the name of Jesus. I destroy the sceptre of the wicked that rests upon the land allotted to me. I boldly declare that the oppressor shall not rest until I possess my possession. I give God praise because He gives me a reason to praise Him for He makes my life full of His abundance.

I am blessed and highly favoured.

REVIVAL

Key Scripture - Habakkuk 3:2

"O LORD, I have heard thy speech, and was afraid: O LORD, revive thy work in the midst of the years, in the midst of the years make known; in wrath remember mercy."

I believe and confess that the move of the Holy Spirit is coming to our city. I give God praise for breaking the hold of the spirit of the antichrist over our city, and putting to shame every evil religion and satanic worship.

I confess that God is softening the heart of His people to seek Him. The heavens are opened to us. These are the days of the latter rain. The Spirit of grace and righteousness shall abound in the land.

I believe and confess that the hold of materialism is broken. The Lord set's us free from the bondage of Egypt. God is ripping all evil from the face of the earth. A new river shall flow. A new hunger, for God shall be manifested in our heart. God will cause His purpose and counsel to stand.

I am blessed and highly favoured.

REWARD

Key Scripture - Proverbs 11:18b

"But to him that soweth righteousness shall be a sure reward."

I believe and confess and give glory to God for His continuous work in my life. I thank the Lord for the great plans which He has for me. I bless His holy name because He began a good work in me and is sure able to complete it.

I boldly confess that the Lord will uphold me in all of my Christian race, He has helped me to begin and I shall finish well. I confess that my journey shall end in obtaining a crown.

I confess by faith that the ability to bring fleshly desires under control has been given to me by the Holy Spirit for the Lord will cause me to be a channel of blessing and He shall give me the grace to focus on the mark of my calling. For the Lords mighty hand shall uphold me in the midst of the challenges of life so that my service in private and in public shall result in divine promotion.

I receive the reward of enduring temptation in the

name of the Lord. I receive the grace not to bow to the pressure of adversity, but rather to stand until I receive divine approval. The grace to serve with integrity rests upon my life. My expectation shall not go unfulfilled for the Lord will make me go into the realms of a full reward in Jesus name. God is causing a transfer of the wealth of the wicked and ungodly to come into my life. My seed sown shall result in a harvest.

I bless the name of the Lord for the reward that is released in my life as I walk in unity with the brethren. I give God praise for all He shall do. He shall overwhelm my life with His blessing and He shall overwhelm my life with His strength.

I am blessed and highly favoured.

SALVATION OF SOULS

KEY SCRIPTURE - ACTS 16:32

"And they spake unto him the word of the Lord, and to all that were in his house."

I give God praise for He is good. He has favoured me with His salvation. I thank God for sending Jesus. I give praise to the Lord for shedding His blood for my redemption.

I confess that my household shall come to know the Lord.

I boldly confess that He will touch my colleagues and friends. I reach forth, by faith and break the hold of the spirit of pride and ignorance that is holding my relations in unbelief. For the Lord will save my household, according to His Word.

By faith I confess that God will use me as a channel for reaching others. He will use me to break the power of legalism, sin, and satan in their lives.

I am blessed and highly favoured.

SATISFACTION

KEY SCRIPTURE - PROVERBS 18:20

"A man's belly shall be satisfied with the fruit of his mouth; and with the increase of his lips shall he be filled."

I believe and confess that the Lord is good, He causes me to have victory at all times. He satisfies my mouth with good things and therefore I confess that the Lord will strengthen me in my moments of weariness and He will make the blessings of the Levites which brings satisfaction to rest upon my life. The presence of the Lord will cause joy to increase in my life.

I confess boldly that the cycle of poverty and lack is broken. I enter into the realm of satisfaction. I thank the Lord for strength in my marrow to bring satisfaction. I give Him praise for causing me to know fulfilment in my work and my commitments.

I boldly confess that success rests on all of my labour. Positive results will always follow everything I do. I give God the praise because I shall be blessed with all of the blessings of heaven for the Lord will cause me to know victory over the cycle of poverty and lack, and He will bring into my life the satisfaction that transcends physical and material advancement.

I boldly confess that the abundance of Gods glory rests on my life, the abundance of Gods mercy increases in me for the Lord will send help to me even in may challenging times. He has promised to satisfy my heart in the time of famine, therefore the Lord will make me a blessing to those who are wounded and make my life to be a challenge to those who are troubled.

I thank the Lord for His peace that passes understanding and flows like a river therefore, I confess that I shall be strengthened to be diligent and productive in my days.

I am blessed and highly favoured.

SECURITY

KEY SCRIPTURE - PROVERBS 18:10

"The name of the LORD is a strong tower: the righteous runneth into it, and is safe."

Give God praise for being my refuge and strength in the time of trouble. I thank the Lord for He is my defence against the enemy's attack; for the Lord will cause me to know His arm of protection at all times and He will cause me to learn to put my trust in His name. I dwell in the land of safety by faith and none shall make me afraid.

I believe and confess that the love and grace of God around me abounds for me. I confess that the Holy Spirit will build and fortify His hedge around me. I am surrounded with the peace of God and therefore, I take authority over every trouble of the night that causes me to fret.

I confess that no weapon of the enemy formed against me prospers and every mouth that rises against me in judgement is condemned. For the angel of the Lord will scatter all those who are plotting against me. He shall uphold me with His mighty power. The name of the Lord becomes my dwelling place, He lifts my hand above that of the enemy and gives me a testimony over every demonic dragon that may be attacking me.

I boldly declare victory over the terror of the night and the evil of darkness. I cover myself from the pestilence of the enemy floating around. I release angelic presence around my home in the name of the Lord.

I am blessed and highly favoured.

SELF-ESTEEM

KEY SCRIPTURE - Philippians 4:13

"I can do all things through Christ which strengtheneth me."

I bless the name of the Lord. I thank my Lord and saviour Jesus Christ for setting me free from the power and bondage of insecurity. I give God praise because every evil pronouncement made into my life, He has turned around for my favour therefore, I break the power of emotional bondage and I loose myself from every tendency to be controlled by the evil one. I declare myself totally free from the bondage of selfishness, self-righteousness and self-pity. I declare that every tendency of self-abuse and self-pity is gone from me in Jesus name.

I boldly declare that God uses me for His glory for I am His new creature, created in Christ Jesus for favour, for glory and for praise.

I am motivated daily to be an achiever. I am finding my value in God for I am bought with a high price. The blood of Jesus cleanses me from all unrighteousness therefore I have victory in the Lord Jesus Christ. Yes, I have dominion over every challenge that I may face.

I am blessed and highly favoured.

SERVING THE LORD

KEY SCRIPTURE - ZEPHANIAH 3:9

"For then will I turn to the people a pure language, that they may all call upon the name of the LORD, to serve him with one consent."

I give God the praise for making me a minister of righteousness. I thank the Lord for the boldness to preach His word even in the most adverse situation. I thank the Lord for the strength to serve Him and not to live in sin.

I boldly confess that the power of God will be manifest in my ministry and that the Lord will confirm His word in my mouth. Like Joseph with Potiphar, my serving will open the doors of grace and favour. I receive by faith divine approval upon my ministry in the name of Jesus.

I believe and confess that the Lord gives me the strength to lay all on the altar of sacrifice and to commit myself totally to His purpose and His counsel. I confess that I shall not serve mammon but the Lord for the Lord will cause my service to result in being rewarded and not rejected in the name of Jesus. I give God the praise for the heart of a servant. I thank the Lord for being able to serve Him with a heart of humility.

I boldly confess that the Lord strengthens me and gives me all that it takes to serve Him even in the most difficult settings.

I am blessed and highly favoured.

SINGLES

Key Scripture - Proverbs 12:14

"A man shall be satisfied with good by the fruit of his mouth: and the recompence of a man's hands shall be rendered unto him."

I give praise to the Lord, the Father of all spirits for counting me worthy to be called His child. I thank the Lord for pulling me out of darkness into His marvellous light.

I confess that I am free from loneliness, fear and bondage. I receive the healing of the Lord for previous hurt and damaging relationships. I am free from emotional damage, and every lie of satan. Rather, every lie of satan shall be exposed to me in the area of marriage. My steps will be ordered of the Lord. For the Lord will bring into my life the person of His choosing. Through Him I shall not fail but succeed in my married life.

I believe and confess that God has a plan for my life; a good plan and not evil. He will cause me to enter His purpose and to rejoice in what He has put in place for me. I give God praise because He is able to handle what ever challenge I face. I boldly declare that my body belongs to God and my mind is ruled by the Holy Spirit. I shall not serve sin but shall walk in the glory of the Lord. I believe and confess that every blessing in the area of marriage which the Lord has for me shall not pass me by.

I release the spouse which God has chosen for my life. I loose my future spouse whom the enemy has caged. I receive into my life the person which God has prepared for me. I rejoice in the Lord because He causes me to have His best. I thank the Lord in advance for sending the person who brings joy into my heart. I reject every curse of divorce in advance and thank the Lord for He will give me a glorious marriage. I boldly declare that I shall not yield to sexual pressure but walk in the purpose and counsel of God.

I am blessed and highly favoured.

STEADFASTNESS

KEY SCRIPTURE - 1 CORINTHIANS 15:58

"Therefore, my beloved brethren, be ye steadfast, unmovable, always abounding in the work of the Lord, forasmuch as ye know that your labour is not in vain in the Lord."

I give God praise because His steadfast love will never ceases. I thank the Lord because He is my anchor who holds me firm during the billows of life.

I believe and confess that the Lord will help me to be steadfast in the things of His kingdom. His grace will be sufficient in moments of discouragement. I boldly confess that my eyes are upon the Lord for He upholds me to run my Christian race to the end.

I confess that as I always hold on to His word, God will cause His blessing and favour to flow towards me. He shall help me to be steadfast in the pursuit of excellence. The Lord will help me to be steadfast in the pursuit of what I confess and overcome whatever challenges I face.

I believe and confess that I receive confidence to flow in the joy of the Lord in the face of distractions and troubles. I receive the joy of the Lord to be able to stand against the attack of the enemy.

I confess that the angels of the Lord surround me and I am able to hold onto my faith during the rough times of this life. I believe and confess that my eyes will remain on the Lord's promises and not the situations.

I confess boldly that when my heart is overwhelmed, I will stand on the promise of the Lord.

I am blessed and highly favoured.

STRENGTH

Key Scripture - Isaiah 41:10

"Fear thou not; for I [am] with thee: be not dismayed; for I am thy God: I will strengthen thee; yea, I will help thee; yea, I will uphold thee with the right hand of my righteousness."

I believe and confess that the Lord is good, He causes me to be strengthened day to day for the Lord is making my life a wall of strength in the land. God causes my life to be like an iron pillar and a brazen wall. My weak moments reveal the power of God. The ability of God to transform my weakness into strength flows into my life.

I receive the strength to be fruitful in my following the Lord. For God causes me to increase in knowledge of His. The Lord strengthens me with all His might and the grace of God is accompanied by patience, long-suffering and joyfulness.

By faith, I prevail with God in prayer. I confess that God becomes my strength and help in the time of need and the power of God in my life will mark His calling on my life. I release the strength of the Lord against the impossible situation I am facing and receive divine breakthrough as I confront every challenge.

I boldly declare, that the anointing to turn back the onslaught of the enemy rests upon me. I confess that irrespective of what I see, His strength shall match my days on earth. The Lord will always be my source of strength. Divine intervention of God in what I am facing will follow at all times in Jesus name.

I declare that God becomes my source of deliverance and causes me to rise above every situation. The nets and traps of the enemy are broken for my sake, the oppression of the enemy is shattered for my sake, I come under the shelter of the almighty God during the attacks of the enemy.

I take refuge under His strength, He becomes my help in my time of need and He will always be there when ever I am faced with challenges.

I am blessed and highly favoured.

THANKSGIVING

Key Scripture - Psalm 50:14

"Offer unto God thanksgiving; and pay thy vows unto the most High:"

Now Thanks be unto God who causes us to have victory at all times through the Lord Jesus Christ. I give thanks to the Lord for His mercy which endures forever. I bless Him for the truth of His word which endures to all generations. The Lord be magnified for the benefit of His salvation which I enjoy in Christ Jesus. I lift up the name of the Lord for forgiving my sins and paying the price for my salvation. I thank the Lord for the work of His healing for my body and total deliverance from the bed of sickness and disease.

I bless the name of the Lord for His strength in making me to live in His glory and crowning my life with His love and kindness. I thank the Lord for His mercy and His grace that has abounded unto me. The Lord be praised for He has obtained mercy on my behalf and has brought victory at all times.

Thanks be to God for the indescribable gift of Jesus Christ, His dear son. Thanks be to God for His promise not to leave nor forsake me. I lift up the name of the Lord because gladness will not seize in my life but, the joy of the Lord shall continue to be my strength and the voice of thanksgiving will perpetually be heard in my household.

I am blessed and highly favoured.

TRANSITION

KEY SCRIPTURE - LEVITICUS 26:4

"Then I will give you rain in due season, and the land shall yield her increase, and the trees of the field shall yield their fruit."

I believe and confess that the Lord is good. I thank the Lord because He has a better time for the manifestation of His favour in my life. I thank Him because He will see me through whatever challenges I am facing. I give God the praise because nothing shall be big enough to stop His love in my heart. I command that there will be a change to the rough seasons that I am going through. By faith, I command a stop to the long seasons of lack in my life and I speak forth the abundance of God's supply in the name of Jesus.

I believe and confess fruitfulness in all areas of my life and at all seasons in the name of Jesus. In my moments of transition, I ask the Lord for the word in season that will guide me; for the Lord, Himself, will use me at all times to touch those who are going through their own transition.

I confess by faith, that I receive strength to wait until

my change comes. I believe and confess that the grace to keep me being zealous for the Lord will continue to abound in my life.

I confess by faith that my transition time shall turn to a time of transformation.

I am blessed and highly favoured.

TRIUMPH

KEY SCRIPTURE - 2 CORINTHIANS 2:14

"Now thanks be unto God, which always causeth us to triumph in Christ, and maketh manifest the savour of his knowledge by us in every place."

I boldly sing to the Lord a song of triumph for His victory over the enemy. I give God praise for helping me to overcome the lies of the devil. I thank my Lord and saviour for His faithfulness to deliver His children from the onslaught of the enemy. For the Lord makes way for me out of every difficult situation.

I confess that I escape every situation set by the enemy for the Lord will frustrate the plans of evil doers and He will cause every journey of the enemy to end in their own Red Sea.

I boldly confess that the oppressor and his weapon will drown in his own Red Sea. I declare by faith, that the children of evil doers shall not overcome me but rather, I shall be triumphant in all that I lay my hands on.

I believe and confess that the enemy shall have no reason to rejoice over me for the Lord will counter every evil imagination of satan against my life and my home.

I believe and confess that I receive breakthrough that will cause a triumphant shout in the house of God on my behalf. I give God praise for causing me to be triumphant at all times over the works of satan, over the attacks of the enemy and over the lies spoken against me.

I boldly confess that the Lord will make a public show of the defeat of the enemy and the victory He is bringing into my life. I command the fury of the Lord to come upon the enemy that seeks my destruction. I declare that I tread upon the enemy and He is under my feet. I thank the Lord for His promise to put the enemy under my feet at all times and to give me victory over everything that rises against me.

My trust is in the Lord and not in my weapons I take authority over every serpentine spirit and declare total victory in the name of Jesus.

I am blessed and highly favoured.

TRUST

KEY SCRIPTURE - PSALM 37:3

"Trust in the LORD, and do good; so shalt thou dwell in the land, and verily thou shalt be fed."

I believe and confess that the Lord has given me the grace and privilege of knowing Him. My heart trusts in the Lord for He has promised to be my help in the time of need.

I shall not lack anything. Fear has no hold over my life. The weapon of discouragement is cancelled, in the Name of Jesus. Each day of my life shall reveal His glory. Because I trust in the Lord, I shall be like Mount Zion which cannot be removed.

I take authority over the weapons of discouragement and cancel them in the name of the Lord. I rejoice because God's grace is sufficient for me at all times. I put my trust in the Lord and I know that I shall not be disappointed. I believe and confess that in the midst of all setbacks, God's grace shall be sufficient for me; my expectation shall not be confounded.

I am blessed and highly favoured.

UNDERSTANDING

Key Scripture - Proverbs 3:19

"The LORD by wisdom hath founded the earth; by understanding hath he established the heavens."

I give God praise for divine understanding. I thank the Lord for insight into situations of life. By faith, I confess that God gives me the grace of understanding of the deep truths of His word. I profit through the entrance of the word of God into my life. I grow in the grace of Jesus Christ to a full understanding of the knowledge of the Father.

I boldly confess that the Lord is my helper and He gives me rich understanding of the person and the working of God. I receive deeper revelation of the person of Christ; a deeper understanding of humans so that I can minister effectively to them. I operate on a higher level of understanding through the Lord Jesus Christ and on a day by day basis. The Lord causes me to increase as I pursue Him. He shall give me a deeper craving for the knowledge of His word and a divine understanding to preserve me from falling into error. I refuse and reject any association with people who crave for the wrong thing.

I confess that every association that will bless me and increase me comes my way. I receive the favour of insight into the deep things of life. I thank the Lord for the safety that comes through the knowledge of His word. I give God praise for the Holy Spirit who opens my eyes to discover the things of God.

I am blessed and highly favoured.

UNITY

Key Scripture - Psalm 133:1

" Behold, how good and how pleasant it is for brethren to dwell together in unity!"

I believe and confess that the Lord is good. His faithfulness is forever more.

I boldly confess that I walk in love, and I receive the grace that keeps the unity of the body of Christ. The spirit of division, hatred and selfishness is far from me. I leave no room for the manifestation of disunity. I give God praise for giving me victory, in Jesus Christ.

I believe and confess that God orders my steps to walk in love and peace with the members of His household. I give God praise for the spirit of unity and love in my household. I rejoice in the Lord for filling my heart with affection towards His children. I take authority over every generational curse connected to me and I set myself free from it and declare boldly that I shall not walk in disunity but walk in love at all times. I confess that the spirit of division shall not operate in my life, in my marriage, church and household. I thank the Lord because unto Him shall the gathering of His people be. The power which flows in the place where there is unity rests upon me.

I am blessed and highly favoured.

VISION

KEY SCRIPTURE - HAbAKKuk 2:2-3

"And the LORD answered me, and said, Write the vision, and make it plain upon tables, that he may run that readeth it.

For the vision is yet for an appointed time, but at the end it shall speak, and not lie: though it tarry, wait for it; because it will surely come, it will not tarry."

I believe and confess that God gives my life the vision necessary to make progress. I thank the Lord for His vision and program for my life. I boldly confess that my eyes are anointed to see God's plan for the future. God gives me insight into the destiny which He has for me. The eyes of my understanding are enlightened, the purpose of my calling are made clear and known to me.

I confess that I will pursue the vision of my life when others do not believe. I confess that the Lord will send people who will understand and believe my vision and He will give me a heart to pursue the purpose for which I have been created.

I believe and confess that I fully possess the vision of God and I progress in it no matter what the size is.

Everything that comes against my vision shall fall for my sake. For the Lord will cause an explosion of the gift of revelation in the midst of my troubles.

I receive a heart of humility in the face of great visions which the Lord shows. I receive clear and divine understanding for life. The Lord, Himself, will cause me to have a clearly defined destination. He shall be my help to carry out His plan for my life. I give God praise in advance for giving me fulfilment in every aspect of life.

I am blessed and highly favoured.

WATCHFULNESS

KEY SCRIPTURE - PROVERBS 8:34

"Blessed is the man that heareth me, watching daily at my gates, waiting at the posts of my doors."

I give God praise who always causes me to have victory in the Lord Jesus Christ. I bless the name of the Lord for His faithfulness to those who trust in Him. I believe and confess that the Lord helps me to be watchful in my Christian life. The Lord open my eyes to the things that hinders and gives me the grace to be an overcomer. The Lord will expose the secret plans of the enemy to me in Jesus name. By faith, I come against the spirit of spiritual slumber and I receive the Lord's help for all situations. I take authority over every demonic eye watching with the intention to do me harm.

I pray by faith and confess that the Lord will surprise me with His promotion. I receive the grace to watch and wait at all times for God's divine order for my life. I bless the name of the Lord for giving me leaders and mentors who watch over my spirit so that I do not stumble.

The Lord causes me to have spiritual insight and watchfulness. He gives me boldness to stand and not compromise with the worldly system around me.

I humble myself before the Lord and resist the works of the enemy. I give God praise for He has promised never to leave me nor forsake me.

I am blessed and highly favoured.

WINNING

Key Scripture - Revelation 12:11

*"And they overcame him by the blood of the Lamb, and
by the word of their testimony; and they loved not their
lives unto the death."*

I believe and confess that the Lord is good for God
causes me to have victory through the Lord Jesus Christ.
I thank the Lord for defeating satan on my behalf in the
name of Jesus. I confess that the blessings of the Lord
will prevail over the challenges that I am facing. I
confess that the hand of the enemy will not prevail
against me. I am victorious over weariness, tiredness and
attack of the enemy.

I confess that I will succeed, for the Lord will make
my life peculiar for Him in the midst of a thousand
people. God will cause me to have victory over sin and
dominion over situations. I believe and confess that I
will eat the good the land. I give God praise for turning
around famine years and making them harvest times. I
bless the name of the Lord because He will bring a
harvest as I sow the one I have.

I thank the name of the Lord because He will put to

shame every attack of the satan. I lean not on my understanding but totally depend on the grace of God. Every project I lay my hands on will result in success.

The Lord will cause every demonic onslaught to be defeated for my sake. The devil will not prevail over my life and all that belongs to me. The word of God will become my blue print for success and He will network me with those who will bless and increase me. I am victorious over problems. My hands are strengthened by the Lord and the voice of winning shall not seize in my household. The favour and the blessing of the Lord rests upon my home, so the hand of opposition fails against me. The Lord will raise me and make me a testimony of His wealth and riches to the glory of His name.

I am blessed and highly favoured.

WORD OF GOD

KEY SCRIPTURE - HEBREWS 4:12

"For the word of God is quick, and powerful, and sharper than any two-edged sword, piercing even to the dividing asunder of soul and spirit, and of the joints and marrow, and is a discerner of the thoughts and intents of the heart."

I thank the Lord for the light which comes through the entrance of His word. I give God the praise for His word which abides in me and helps me to shape my future.

I thank the Lord for making me enjoy His good word, and for upholding me through His word.

I boldly confess that the word works for me. I am who the word says I am. I receive what the word of God says I have. I become who the word of God says I become. I speak the word of faith that is in me, and I prophesy by faith to every situation I face. The entrance of God's word brings light to me and imparts understanding to my life. I receive the boldness to declare God's word to others, the grace to be a doer of it, and the ability to be victorious over satan through the word.

I am blessed and highly favoured.

WORK

KEY SCRIPTURE - DEUTERONOMY 26:15

"Look down from thy holy habitation, from heaven, and bless thy people Israel, and the land which thou hast given us, as thou swarest unto our fathers, a land that floweth with milk and honey."

I give God the praise for the opportunity to be alive and healthy today I thank the Lord for access to His throne through the Lord Jesus Christ. I bless the name of the Lord for proving Himself mighty and strong on my behalf. I confess that the Lord causes me to have opportunity to touch humanity with His blessings and abilities that are in my life.

I am a blessing to those who come near me, who work under me and to my colleagues. I take authority over the spirit of disunity and betrayal from entering my business and my work in the name of Jesus. No evil befalls me and no danger comes near my working or dwelling place. The Lord will make me an example of His glory at work. He will cause me to shine as light in this crooked world.

I thank the Lord in advance because my labour will

not be in vain. God, Himself, will manifest His blessing and favour upon me and command fruitfulness on every venture I carry out. I take authority over sickness that tries to hinder me from achieving my vision. I bring hindrances to my business or work under me and cancel all such hindrance in the name of Jesus. I receive breakthrough in the area of my income in the name of Jesus.

I bless the name of the Lord because He causes me to increase. All that I have is covered with the blood of Jesus. All that I have increases for me. I give God praise for His faithfulness in all things in Jesus name.

I am blessed an highly favoured.

WORRY-FREE LIVING

KEY SCRIPTURE - Philippians 4:6

"Be careful for nothing; but in every thing by prayer and supplication with thanksgiving let your requests be made known unto God."

I believe and confess that the Lord is good. I give God praise for giving me victory at all times. I bless the name of the Lord for the Spirit of satisfaction and the joy of knowing Jesus. I believe and confess that the Lord has set me free from the spirit of discouragement. I am totally free from unnecessary worry and holding on to the hurts of the past. The peace of God that passes understanding keeps my mind in all circumstances. The peace of God keeps my mind in the night seasons of life. The spirit of fear is bound from me. The tendency to be fearful, have panic attacks and the fear of failure is removed from me. The Lord, Himself, destroys the yoke of the enemy and removes the burden of satan.

I confess that God's peace which passes understanding, keeps my mind: I have the assurance of The Lord being with me in all situations of life. I place all my worries on Christ for He cares for me. I live my life to the glory of God. I am led day by day by the Holy Spirit. No evil befalls me; no danger comes near my dwelling place. Everything I see, hear or feel is all subject to the Holy Spirit. I am totally free from the impact and control of worry.

I am blessed and highly favoured.

WORSHIP

Key Scripture - Revelation 19:6

*"And I heard as it were the voice of a great multitude,
and as the voice of many waters, and as the voice of
mighty thunderings, saying, Alleluia: for the Lord God
omnipotent reigneth."*

I give God praise for His majestic splendour that is
revealed around us. I exalt the Lord who reigns in
majesty and covers Himself with glory. The Lord is
exalted for He is eternal, without a beginning or an end. I
worship Him and magnify His name for He is all
sufficient and needs no one to exist. God is great and
abundant in mercy, kindness, goodness and benevolence.
I bow before Him who dwells in unapproachable light
and magnify His name for He is holy and an all
consuming fire.

The name of the Lord is exalted for He is my source
of salvation, protection and healing. I give praise to the
Lord for His awesomeness. I bless the name of God
because He knows all things: past, present and the future.
He is the omnipresent God who is everywhere. He is the
omnipotent and is all powerful. I rejoice for the privilege
to have a relationship with Him. I thank the Lord for His

goodness which brings His providential care.

I thank God for His grace which He bestows on the undeserving and which cannot be earned. I magnify the name of the Lord for He is worthy to be praised and the fruit of my lips shall continually be His praise. I worship Him because He has revealed Himself as my mighty warrior. His work is perfect and all His ways are just. The works of His hands is marvellous. He is my rock in a weary land. He has the whole world in His hands and subdues all things and therefore, I am not afraid for there is none beside Him, for none can kill and make alive, none can make rich or poor. The earth is the Lords' and the fullness thereof and He is worthy to be exalted.

I am blessed and highly favoured.

ZEAL

KEY SCRIPTURE - 2 PETER 3:14

"Wherefore, beloved, seeing that ye look for such things, be diligent that ye may be found of him in peace, without spot, and blameless."

I thank the Lord for the privilege of serving in His kingdom. I bless the name of the Lord for His great plan for my life. By faith I confess that the Lord gives me the boldness to declare His word. He fills my heart with the sense of urgency to preach His word. My eyes are opened to see the needs of men and preach the word of God.

I receive boldness and anointing of the Holy Spirit to operate with holy zeal for God has given me the heart of a servant for effective ministry. I shall pursue that which has been committed unto my hands and the Lord shall cause me to have good success. The Lord will give me a heart willing to serve Him and He shall seal my ministry with His blessing and His anointing.

By faith, I receive the blessing of zealousness and commitment to the things of God and I confess that I shall make an impact which cannot be erased for the all consuming zeal from the presence of the Lord shall be upon my life and I shall be a blessing to my generation.

I am blessed and highly favoured.

Who I am in Christ

I am a new creature, born of God, into God's family. I am always abounding, because I have all sufficiency in all things, and abound unto every good work. I am a person who lets the peace of God rule in my heart and mind. Therefore, I am carefree about anything. Anxiety and worry do not dominate me. I choose to walk and dwell in the love of God, because I am born of God, filled with the love of God. I am a branch of the true vine. I am a member of the body of Christ.

I am rooted and grounded in the love of God, with my light shining bright. For the Lord Jesus calls me the light of the world, a city that cannot be hidden. I am an imitator of Jesus Christ, set free from the law of sin and death. I am blessed at all times, and I continually praise the Lord, because He has filled my mouth with thanksgiving.

I am accepted in the beloved, free from condemnation, delivered from the evils of this present world. I am born of God, therefore, I am born of love, and I walk and dwell in love. I am an overcomer, through the blood of the Lamb and the word of my testimony. Daily, I overcome the devil, and, therefore, refuse to be moved by what I see. I am a labourer with the Lord.

I am the righteousness of God in Christ, therefore, I am complete in Him. I have been transformed by the renewing of my mind, and so I bring every thought into captivity. I cast down all imaginations, and everything that exhalts itself against the knowledge of Christ. I have the capacity to bring my body into subjection.

By faith I walk with God and not by sight. I call those things that are not seen as though they were. I call into existence things by faith. I am established in the will of God, possessing my confession. Through Christ, I am more than a conqueror. I choose to be above only and not beneath. I am delivered from the power of darkness, translated into the kingdom of Jesus Christ. I am His sheep. The Lord is my shepherd. He leads me and He guides me in the pathway of life. I am led of the Spirit of God, so I shall not miss my way. His Word calls me son. That's who I am.

I am kept in safety wherever I go. Getting all my needs met through Jesus Christ. I cast all my cares upon the Lord, choosing to be strong in the Lord and in the power of His might. For, my Beloved is mine and I am His. I delight myself in the Lord Jesus Christ. I acknowledge Him as the Author of all things. I am a heir of God and a joint heir with Jesus Christ. I can do all things through Christ Who strengthens me. I choose to sit in the heavenly places in Christ Jesus, declaring that I am a heir to the blessing of Abraham.

I choose to observe and to do the Lord's commandment. I am blessed in my going out, and blessed in my coming in. For I have inherited eternal life. So I am blessed with all spiritual blessings, speaking the truth with love, growing up into Jesus Christ in all things. For I am crucified with Christ. I am dead with Christ. I am buried with Christ, and I have risen with Him. I am a blood washed, blood cleansed, blood sanctified child of God. My sins are forgiven.

I am saved by grace. I am born again. I am justified fully through Calvary's love. I have been co-opted into the family of God. So I am a new creature. I am God's workmanship, a partaker of God's divine nature, pure, holy, sanctified. I am in His hand, therefore, I shall not be afraid what man can do to me. His Word says I am redeemed from the curse of the law, for Christ has been made a curse for me. I am healed by His stripes. No disease or sickness, virus; be it genetic or environmental, reigns over my body. My body belongs to God. I am prosperous, reigning in life through Jesus Christ, receiving daily the power to get wealth. I am above principalities and powers, and they are under my feet. Because of Jesus, I exercise authority over the enemy. And, therefore, I am victorious. More than a conqueror, winning every day. Established on earth to reign with Jesus Christ.